1 CORINTHIANS ANNUAL BIBLE STUDY

1 CORINTHIANS
GROWING THROUGH DIVERSITY

DON & ANITA FLOWERS

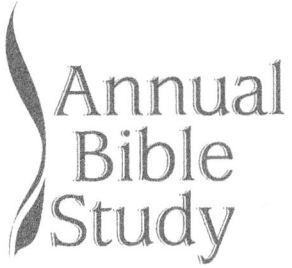
Study Guide

SMYTH&HELWYS
PUBLISHING, INCORPORATED — MACON, GEORGIA

CONTENTS

Cecil P. Staton, Jr.
President & CEO

P. Keith Gammons
Publisher / Executive Vice President

Leslie Andres
Editor

Kelley F. Land
Assistant Editor

Katie Brookins
Associate Editor

Daniel Emerson
Dave Jones
Graphic Design

Sidebar material has been adapted from Robert Scott Nash, *1 Corinthians*, Smyth & Helwys Bible Commentary (Macon GA: Smyth & Helwys, 2009).

1-800-747-3016 (USA)
1-800-568-1248 (Canada)

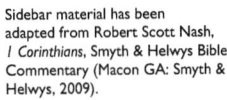

Introduction: A Man, a Church, a Letter, and Us 1

Session 1: Divisions in the Church?
(1 Cor 1:10-17; 3:1-22; 11:17-22) 11

Session 2: Since You Asked
(1 Cor 7:1-16; 8:1-13; 9:16-23; 10:23-33) 21

Session 3: We Have These Different Gifts
(1 Cor 12–14) 33

Session 4: The End Is the Beginning
(1 Cor 15–16) 43

ACKNOWLEDGMENTS

Sometimes the story behind a book is almost more fascinating than the book itself! This may be one of those cases. The editors at Smyth & Helwys invited us to explore the world of 1 Corinthians, a church full of diversity and turmoil and conflict, and to create their Annual Bible Study. We turned to two very different churches to help us along the way.

Providence Baptist Church, at less than two decades old, is a relatively young congregation (especially in Charleston where we have churches that date back to the 1600s!). Providence is a place that continually welcomes diverse opinions, explores different ways of worship, and even agrees to be guinea pigs for the creation of a book. The members of Providence participated with grace and questions and suggestions that helped in the planning and research of this study.

When it came time to write, another congregation offered a place. The Gateway Community Center in Sanur, Bali, invited us to come and be with them for several weeks. This is, by far, the most diverse congregation we have ever been a part of. Individuals from all over the world gather for worship each week with accents from Bali, Indonesia, China, Australia, France, Holland, England, and the list goes on; we spent time with people whose theologies were more Calvinistic than Calvin and people who also pray at the Hindu temple nearby. Worshipers are united by a common language—English—and an experience with the risen Christ. They continue to live out the diversity that was so evident in Corinth. But while we were there, our computers—with our notes and research—were stolen! We pray that the culprits enjoyed the study! To say that the writing process was set back would be an understatement. This is the reconstructed version.

Through it all, Keith Gammons has been an encouraging voice. His belief in us along with his "forced" flexibility has been gift. Leslie Andres has been patient, making our words concise and clear.

Different churches, different situations, different theologies, different writing styles—this book has been an exercise in diversity, the core issue facing Paul and the people of Corinth. Together we have muddled through, hopefully discovering the grace of God along the way.

INTRODUCTION: A MAN, A CHURCH, A LETTER, AND US

It was fall break, and I desperately needed it! I was in my third year of seminary, with papers to write and exams to study for, but I had other things on my mind. My fiancée and I were getting married in a couple of short months, and we had many things to do and many decisions to make.

I arrived at Anita's house before she got home from work. Her mother greeted me and pointed me to my room in the basement. As I made my way through the kitchen, I noticed a letter lying face up on the table. It immediately caught my attention.

Dear Ms Fraley:

I enjoyed our recent conversation. On behalf of all of us at the Peace Corps, let me offer our congratulations on your upcoming marriage. In response to your question, yes, we do appoint married couples. We would suggest that you wait a few months to make the transition into married life and then contact us. There are several opportunities which I believe would be a good fit for you and your fiancé.

Again, congratulations, and I look forward to hearing from you soon.

Sincerely,
The Peace Corps

In all honesty, I knew that Anita had considered joining the Peace Corps before we started dating, but that was *then*! With all the duties surrounding the wedding, we hadn't had a conversation about *now*. Worst of all, she wasn't there at the time so she could talk with me about the letter. I lacked a lot of details. And Anita wouldn't be home from work for at least a few hours.

I was left with a letter that wasn't written to me, but it was about me. It affected me.

Something similar happens when we turn to the letters of Paul. We are spying, peeping over the shoulder of someone who isn't even here. We are reading his mail. And if we aren't cautious, we can come to a conclusion about what is going on that is different from what Paul originally intended.

As we begin to study 1 Corinthians, we have to remember that Paul was writing a letter. He was not sitting in the city of Ephesus thinking, "I need to use caution. I'm writing holy Scripture." If he was, my guess is that he might have been more careful with what he was writing. What would you write if you knew that, 2,000 years later or even 2 years later, your e-mail would be viewed as the holy word of God?

Paul was writing a letter. We must keep that in mind. It was a letter from a particular person to a certain group of people in a situation that was well known to them. The first readers shared certain assumptions, ideas, and relationships. To understand what 1 Corinthians meant to them and what it means to us, we have to consider the letter's original context.

WHO IS PAUL?

Mention Paul, and you will probably get an immediate reaction from people who are familiar with him. On one hand, he is perhaps the most influential person in the history of Christianity. Some say that he is the creator of Christianity, moving it from a cult of Judaism to a world religion. At the very least, Paul wrote the majority of what we know as the New Testament.

Others, however, see him as one who perverted Christ's message, transforming a way of life into a structured religion. He is accused of being a chauvinist who even today influences the position of women in our world.

The truth, as is often the case, lies somewhere between the extremes. Paul is a controversial figure, but his influence cannot be underestimated. This makes it even more surprising that we know relatively little about his birth or his early life. We don't know with certainty when and how he died.

Even the facts we know are hard to reconcile. When we first meet Paul in the Scriptures, he is known as Saul, an aggressive persecutor of Christians. In Acts 7, we learn of a young man named Saul who was present at the stoning of Stephen (Acts 7:54–8:1). Saul was "wreaking havoc against" the early Christian church, throwing both male and female believers into prison (Acts 8:1-3).

Then, in Acts 9, we read about the blinding light Saul encountered on the road to Damascus. At the time, he was "still breathing threats and murder against the disciples of the Lord," and he had asked the high priests for letters to the synagogues at Damascus so that he might find and punish followers of Jesus. On his way to Damascus, he was struck down and saw the light from heaven. A voice asked him, "Why do you persecute me?" Saul's traveling companions saw nothing but heard the voice. The voice of Jesus told Saul to get up and enter the city, where he would be told what to do. Saul's companions led their now-blind leader into Damascus, and the disciple Ananias visited him there. When Ananias laid his hands on Saul, scales fell from Saul's eyes, and he was a believer.

Saul immediately became active in the Damascus church. After many days, we are told that he went to Jerusalem to be a part of the church there, but he got a cool reception from the disciples, who avoided him out of fear and doubt. You can imagine the questionable regard they would give a man who only weeks earlier had been on a campaign to murder and imprison believers.

When Paul writes about his conversion in Galatians 1:13-24, he does not mention a blinding light. He goes to great lengths to declare his independence from the church in Jerusalem, stating that he was ordained by God and did not confer with "any human being" (v. 16). After his calling, he went to Arabia, and only went to meet with the apostles in Jerusalem after three years.

Two different Scriptures. Two different stories.

Thus, the facts we think we know about Paul raise as many questions as they answer. We know that he was from Tarsus. In the first century, Tarsus was one of the large cities of the Eastern Mediterranean. Located on the southeastern coast of what is now Turkey, Tarsus was the capital of Cilicia. Cilicia was divided into two distinctly different areas. The rugged mountain coastline on the west was a notorious hideout for pirates. The eastern part of Cilicia was a smooth, fertile plain. Tarsus was situated on the river Cydnos, with access to a mountain pass known as the Cilician Gates. It was a seaport where goods and people could travel inland. Rome annexed this Greek city in 67 BCE.

Tarsus was where Antony met Cleopatra. It was a major area of intrigue and conflict within the Roman Empire following the death of Julius Caesar. The position of Tarsus as a major seaport and trade center led to a diverse population. Ancient writers speak of its residents as "pirates, seafarers and worshippers of Mithras."[1] We hear echoes of these pirates and philosophers in the ancient writings of Plutarch and Strabo:[2]

> The pirates first grew strong in Cilicia, and were elusive. But then, when the Romans were engaged in civil war, they grew bold and began to attack not just ships at sea, but islands and cities along the coast as well. More hateful than fear they inspired was their extravagance—with gilded masts and purple sails and silver-plated oars. They were a disgrace to Roman supremacy—with drunken revels on every shore. (Plutarch, *Pompey* 24)

> Among the men of Tarsus the zeal for philosophy and other kinds of education surpasses that in Athens and Alexandria and any other place renowned for schools and occupation in philosophy. (Strabo, *Geography* 14.5.13)

Tarsus was a center of Mithraic worship, a religion that believed in the unconquered sun. They held a feast day every year on December 25, which they believed was the winter solstice. A distinctive feature of Mithraic worship was a baptism in which initiates stood under a platform on which a bull was slain. The people below were bathed in the blood that spilled down. They believed that this act symbolized the transfer of life and power to the followers.

Paul was born a Roman citizen. Living in an outpost of the empire, this would have been a privilege given to his parents, perhaps in return for housing troops over the winter. At that time, it was also possible to purchase one's citizenship for 500 drachmae—the equivalent of two years wages for the average day laborer.[3]

In spite of his environment, Paul was a Jew. In his letter to the Philippian church (Phil 3:5), he spells out his pedigree: circumcised on the eighth day, a member of the people of Israel, of the tribe of Benjamin, a Pharisee. Some scholars are confused by Paul's assertion that he was a Pharisee. In Pharisaical education, most students read the Hebrew Scriptures, but Paul seems to have read from the Septuagint.

The Septuagint was the Greek translation of the Hebrew Scriptures. The legend is that seventy-two scribes wrote it in seventy-two days—and they agreed on every detail! The truth is that it evolved over several centuries, and the faithfulness of the translation varies from book to book. The Septuagint became the Scriptures for common people, not for elite scholars.

There are differences between the Hebrew texts and the Septuagint, however, and some are rather significant. Certain Greek ideas creep into the text of the Septuagint. God seems to reflect a Greek bias. The personal names for

God found in the Hebrew Scripture, Yahweh and Elohim disappear and become the abstraction "theos," god, in the Septuagint. There is a trend toward abstraction. In the Hebrew Scripture story of God's call to Moses, Moses is instructed to tell the Hebrews that "I Am has sent me" (Exod 3:14). In the Septuagint, this reads, "the being has sent me."

These may seem like minor changes, but they reflect the incursion of Greek philosophy into the text. They indicate a shift in the very nature of God, as Yahweh becomes the self-existent one, the absolute, the cosmic divine being of Greek philosophy.

The Septuagint also shows an acceptance of polytheism. In Exodus 22:28, the Hebrew text says, "You shall not revile Elohim." The Septuagint broadens this to say, "You shall not revile the gods."[4] In a polytheistic world, this slight but significant shift could lead to a toleration of other gods.

The Septuagint was the Scripture that Paul heard and read. It was a part of his religious DNA, just as the King James Version of the Bible is a part of many people today. Some of us learned memory verses from the King James Version, and so when we hear someone read Psalm 23 from a different translation, it seems strange and different.

Another fact we know about Paul is that he was a tentmaker. It was his profession, how he made his livelihood, how he afforded his missionary journeys. We don't consider this strange today. Paul was one of the original bi-vocational ministers.

In his day, being a tentmaker would have made him suspect. Tents were often made from pigskins. While Jews weren't strictly forbidden to handle pigs, rabbis writing just a few hundred years later suggest that it was a questionable activity for devout Jews. In the Mishnah, we read the story of a man who died and left a brother who was a tanner. His wife pleaded that she should not be forced to marry him as was custom, and her plea was granted. If a Jewish man became a tanner, that was grounds for his wife to divorce him.[5]

So we know that Paul was a Roman citizen born in a center of Mithraic worship who was a Jewish tentmaker and also a self-proclaimed Pharisee who read from the Septuagint. These seemingly self-contradictory characteristics add to the mystery of Paul, but they also explain how he has been able to transcend many barriers in both the ancient and modern worlds.

WHAT ABOUT CORINTH?

Corinth was a Greek city, located on the Isthmus of Corinth and overlooking the ports of Cenchreae and Lechaeum. Its location made it an important east-west trade route between the Aegean and Ionian seas. Traders would avoid sailing around the dangerous Peloponnesian peninsula by stopping at one port and sending their cargo overland to the other side. Small ships were often carted across the four-and-a-half-mile isthmus.

The other distinguishing characteristic of Corinth was that is served as the home of the Isthmian Games. Held every two years, this athletic competition was second only to the Olympic games. The games brought in large crowds and were a major source of revenue for the city. The importance of this event can be

Map of the Corinthia

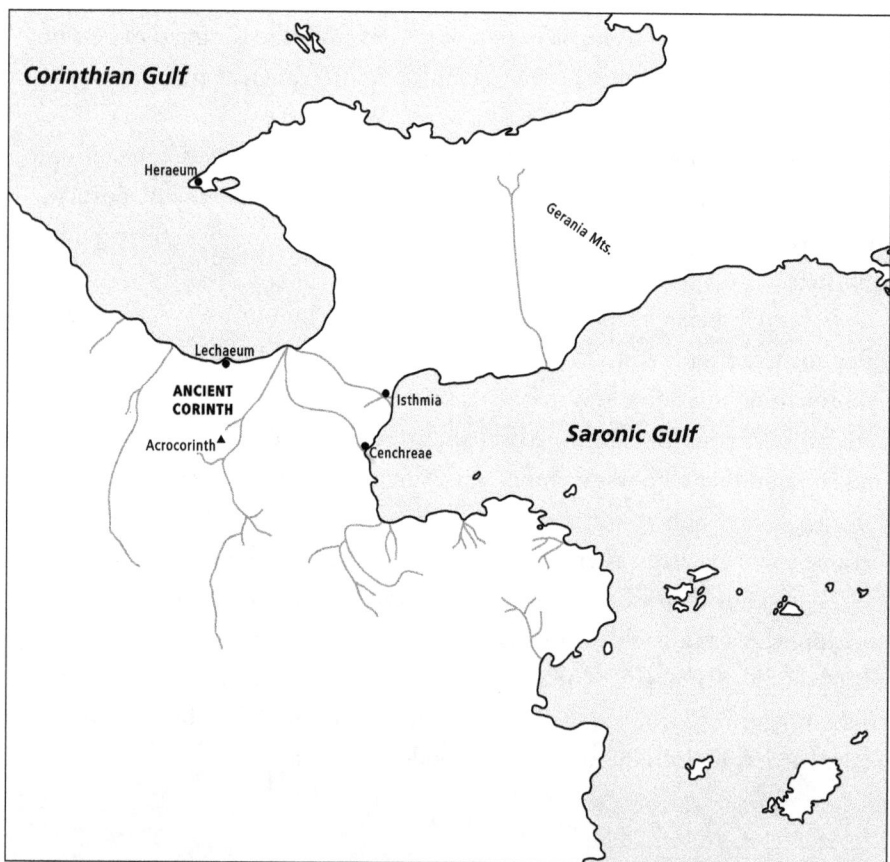

seen in the fact that the most prestigious political office in Corinth was the sponsor of the games.

The economic life of the city was interrupted in 146 BCE when the Romans took the city. They destroyed the buildings, captured and/or enslaved the inhabitants, and basically left the city abandoned until 44 BC, when Julius Caesar reestablished the city. Most of the new colonists were former slaves who discovered not only freedom but also an opportunity for economic advancement.

The city is still known as a center of sexual immorality. "Old Corinth" had such a reputation for sexual vice that Aristophanes coined the term "*korinthiaz*," meaning to act like a Corinthian, or to commit fornication.

Isthmia

Ruins of the sanctuary of Poseidon on the isthmus of Corinth, facing east. (Credit: Scott Nash)

The sanctuary of Poseidon on the isthmus of Corinth was the site of one of the four Panhellenic festivals that featured competitions. The Isthmian games were held in the spring of the second and fourth years of the Panhellenic cycle; the Olympic games were held in the summer of the first year, the Pythian games at Delphi in the summer of the third year, and the Nemean games in the summer of the second and fourth years. In the Roman period and perhaps earlier, the Isthmian contests were held in honor of the dead boy-hero Melikertes-Palaimon.

Elizabeth R. Gebhard, "The Isthmian Games and the Sanctuary of Poseidon in the Early Empire," in *The Corinthia in the Roman Period* (ed. Timothy E. Gregory; JRASup 8: Ann Arbor MI: Journal of Roman Archaeology, 1993) 78–94.

Helmut Koester, "Melikertes at Isthmia: A Roman Mystery Cult," in *Greeks, Romans, and Christians: Essays in Honor of Abraham J. Malherbe* (ed. David L. Balch, Everett Ferguson, and Wayne A. Meeks; Minneapolis: Fortress Press, 1990) 355–66.

Recent scholarship has shown that this perspective was not accurate. Sexual sin was undoubtedly present in the city, but it was expected in any seaport where money flowed freely and men and women were available.[6] C. K. Barrett has said that Corinth was probably a little better and a little worse than any other seaport and commercial center of the day.[7] Today, we would probably imagine a combination of New York, Los Angeles, and Las Vegas!

Like any major city, Corinth offered its citizens many options for worship. Archaeologists have uncovered temples to Apollo, Venus, Isis, and Demeter as well as "the synagogue of the Hebrews."[8] Because of that variety, the members of the church in Corinth would have been tempted by the theologies floating around.

The Corinthian church was a stew of these populations. In his writing, Paul seems to go out of his way to emphasize the diversity of the church—Jew, Greek, slave, and free (1 Cor 12:13). Of the people named in 1 Corinthians, at least three are Jewish; three or four have Roman names; at least one has some wealth, while others were slaves or had little in the way of financial security.[9]

While some members of the church came from a Jewish background, it is apparent that among the congregants were former idol worshipers and others who were drawn to the community for a variety of reasons. They shared no central theology, philosophy, or denominational background. Nothing in particular held them together. As such, Paul spends much of the letter reminding them of what he taught them and correcting the mash-up of various theologies and philosophies.

WHAT IS A LETTER?

In our world of e-mail, Facebook, Twitter, Pinterest, Skype, cell phones, text messages, and twenty-four-hour news channels, it is hard to remember a time when sending or receiving a handwritten letter was a major event. In the ancient world, information was shared via letters—whether they involved family relationships, diets, theological treatises, or the fall of an empire.

Ancient letters were written on just about everything! Letters have been discovered on papyrus but also on clay potsherds. A wooden postcard-size document was uncovered that details the lives of Roman soldiers around Hadrian's Wall in northern England. Kings and emperors had couriers to deliver their letters. Wealthy individuals might have sent slaves with their correspondence. For most, however, letters had to wait until travelers were heading in that direction.

Writing a letter was an adventure. Not everyone knew how to write. The elite had secretaries, while others had to employ scribes to write for them. Nor was it assured that the recipient could read. There might be difficulties in reading the handwriting, translating the text, or other issues that the letter carrier would have to try to handle.

It appears that 1 Corinthians gives us a bit of all the above.

While our Bible names this correspondence First Corinthians, we need to remember that we are coming into the middle of a conversation. This is neither the first nor the last letter that Paul sent the church in Corinth. Even though our Bible contains Second Corinthians, it is apparent from reading it that some letters from Paul are lost, and perhaps others have been folded into the Scriptures we have.

Paul had helped found the church at Corinth and had stayed there several years before moving to Ephesus. While in Ephesus, he wrote a letter to the Corinthian church that is now lost but is referred to in 1 Corinthians 5:9. The letter we know as 1 Corinthians is a response to a letter from the church. Paul seems taken aback by the people's exceptions and their questions about some of his teachings. The situation is made worse (or better) by what he heard from Chloe's people, who had delivered the letter.

The task for Paul is to reassert his authority while changing the theology and behavior of a group of questioning, diverse believers. This was not an easy task in the ancient world, and it isn't easy in our world, either! While we don't have all the information, we do get to read over Paul's shoulder and imagine him writing to us and to our church. This letter isn't *to* us, but it is *about* us.

NOTES

1. A. N. Wilson, *Paul: The Mind of the Apostle* (New York: Norton Press, 1997) 25.

2. "In the Footsteps of Paul," *Peter and Paul and the Christian Revolution*, PBS.org, http://www.pbs.org/empires/peterandpaul/ (accessed 3 October 2013).

3. Wilson, *Paul,* 29.

4. Calvin J. Roetzel, *The Letters of Paul: Conversations in Context* (Louisville KY: Westminster John Knox, 2009) 21.

5. Wilson, *Mind of the Apostle,* 31.

6. Gordon D. Fee, *The First Epistle to the Corinthians* (Grand Rapids MI: Eerdmans, 1987) 3.

7. Cited in Richard B. Hayes, *First Corinthians* (Louisville KY: Westminster John Knox, 1997) 4.

8. Pheme Perkins. First Corinthians (Grand Rapids MI: Baker Academics, 2012) 12–13.

9. Fee, *First Epistle to the Corinthians,* 3.

Session 1

DIVISIONS IN THE CHURCH?

Focal Text: 1 Corinthians 1:10-17; 3:1-22; 11:17-22

On a sunny spring day, go to a graduation ceremony at any seminary or divinity school in the country. Walk up to any graduate, and between the pictures and the hugs and the well wishes, ask what she expects to discover in the church she's heading to. Her answers might resemble those you would get from your congregation if you asked them to describe the church of their dreams.

"A church where everyone loves each other."
"A church where everyone is welcomed."
"A church where the needs of individuals are met."
"A church where people come to know the depth of life."
"A church where worship is moving and the preaching is great."
"A church where people meet Jesus."
"A church where the bills are paid." (There is always one realist in the mix!)

But soon after arriving at their new church, most young ministers will be hit with reality. It is not all sweetness and harmony. There are conflicts in paradise. And the causes vary.

"The Mother's Morning Out program used our glue again!"
"Who thought it would be a good idea to rent a bus to take the kids to camp?"
"I think we need to cut the education budget so we can give more to missions" (or vice versa).
"We've been in this Sunday school classroom for fifty years! I don't see why we have to move now."

"I think it's inappropriate for that girl to serve Communion wearing flip-flops."

"What does the pastor do on her day off, anyway?"

"I think they should do more to help out around here."

"Are we having Communion again? We just *had* Communion!"

Does any of this sound familiar? (Not in your church, of course, but the one you used to go to across town.)

The reality is that churches large and small deal with conflict. It comes at budget time, with personnel, with theology and worship style, and with the décor of the sanctuary and classrooms. The problem is not just with the local church; *the* church as a whole is conflicted. Denominations are breaking apart over disagreements about missions and women and homosexuality and budgets.

At times, we want to throw our hands up and scream, "Can't we just get along?" Given the level of discord, we can understand why the fastest-growing religious group in our country is the "Nones"—those who claim no religious affiliation.

We dream of a time when the church was like our dreams, the way that Jesus wanted it to be. But it was never that way. Pay attention to the great hymn that we sing in church, "The Church's One Foundation." We nod our heads through the first verse:

> The church's one foundation is Jesus Christ our Lord;
> we are his new creation by water and the Word;
> from heaven he came and sought us to be his holy bride;
> with his own blood he bought us, and for our life he died.

One foundation! We are all united. We are one in the Lord. But if we continue singing, we come to a verse that begins, "Though with a scornful wonder the world sees us oppressed, by schisms rent asunder, by heresies distressed . . . ."

But wait! How can folks in the church with one foundation be rent asunder and distressed by heresies?

It is true. And, in fact, it has always been true. There was never a church free of conflict—at least not after the second member joined. Conflict happens. It happened in Corinth for many of the same reasons we face today. It would have been easier if the dissension was organized, but it was legion. There were multiple issues then, just as there are today.

The conflicts seem to catch Paul off guard. It seems that he had intended to write a letter filled with love and accolades. As soon as he finishes his traditional ancient written greeting, which is flowery and ornate, he sings the praises of the people in Corinth:

> I thank my God always for you, because of God's grace that was given to you in Christ Jesus. That is, you were made rich through him in everything: in all your communication and every kind of knowledge, in the same way that the testimony about Christ was confirmed with you. The result is that you aren't missing any spiritual gift while you wait for our Lord Jesus Christ to be revealed. He will also confirm your testimony about Christ until the end so that you will be blameless on the day of our Lord Jesus Christ. God is faithful, and you were called by him to partnership with his Son, Jesus Christ our Lord. (1 Cor 1:4-9)

"I thank my God always...." What a strong and encouraging statement! It sets the tone for what Paul wants to write.

But it seems that he never got a chance. Perhaps he had just written those words when Chloe's people arrived with a response to an earlier letter he had sent, full of questions asking for clarification. Even more, Chloe's people were able to fill in the blanks, giving Paul the scoop about was actually happening in Corinth. Suddenly, the tone of the letter

Rembrandt's Paul

Rembrandt. *The Apostle Paul*. c. 1657. Oil on canvas. The National Gallery of Art, Washington D.C.

Rembrandt has depicted Paul as somber and contemplative, with a hint of strain in his face, taking pen in hand to write one of his letters. Considering the host of problems Paul had to address in 1 Corinthians, one might suspect that Rembrandt had this epistle in mind.

changes. Paul can't keep going with love and accolades. There are conflicts to address.

WHOSE SIDE ARE YOU ON?

In a previous life, I was a youth minister in an established church with a long history. In my new life, I am the first pastor of Providence Baptist Church on Daniel Island. As I was getting ready to leave my youth minister job, I led sessions with our teenagers that focused on points I wanted to be sure they heard me say. I was in the middle of a serious conversation when one of the young men raised his hand and asked, "Don, you're going to be the first pastor of this church, right?" I assured him that was the case and went back to the serious conversation.

"So, years from now," he continued, "when that church puts up the pictures of all the pastors like we have in the hallway, your picture will be the first one?"

I hadn't thought about this, but I agreed with his thinking. Before I could get started again, however, he stated, "Have you ever noticed how ugly they are?"

And that was the end of our serious conversation.

But the young man was right—not about the pictures being ugly but about how every minister lives in the shadow of those who came before. They are always compared to other ministers people have known. They are compared to the idealized minister the church hopes to have.

This happened to Paul. He had founded the church in Corinth and nurtured the fledgling congregation, but the time came when he needed to go to other mission fields. Though he loved the church, there were other congregations to start and other ministries to birth.

The church in Corinth was not left alone. Other ministers came to be among them. There were evangelists and missionaries who passed through, sharing their wisdom, theology, gifts, and ideas. Just as they do today, some had more appeal than others.

How many of us can remember a minister from our past who epitomized everything we knew to be "right" about a minister? "The way she preached was incredible!" "He had a way with senior adults!" "Do you remember the time he cooked chili for everyone on Wednesday night?" "I will never forget how she was with me when my husband died."

Sometimes such exclamations are followed with, "We haven't had anyone like that since!"

But often, when the new minister arrives, people fall in love with him or her. "She's such a wonderful preacher!" "I can finally understand what this preacher is saying!" "I love the fact that people are starting to join our church now that our new minister is here!"

That was happening in Corinth, too. In 1 Corinthians 1:12-13, we hear names of other teachers. Since Paul's departure, there had been a series of other preachers who had come, namely Apollos. According to Acts 18:24-28, Apollos was a learned Jew from Alexandria "who taught accurately the things about Jesus." He was an eloquent and passionate speaker, and "he was of great help to those who had come to believe through grace" (vv. 25, 27). He had an audience who admired him and the way he presented the gospel.

There was yet another group with an agenda and opinions. These were the "back-to-basics" folks who wanted to return to the original apostles. Some in the church at Corinth followed Cephas, the Aramaic name for Peter (Matt 18:8). There is no evidence that Peter had

Paul and Peter
Though no evidence exists that Peter (Cephas) ever visited Corinth, the tradition (based on 1 Cor 1:12) that he did is maintained in the Catholic and Orthodox churches. By placing the two apostles flanked by Corinthian column capitals, Bagnacavallo may have intended his drawing to depict their joint ministry there.

Bagnacavallo (dit), Ramenghi Bartolomeo l'Ancien (1485–1542). *St. Peter and St. Paul*. Pen & brown ink, wash, black chalk on beige paper. Louvre, Paris, France. Photo: Jean-Gilles Berizzi. (Credit: Réunion des Musées Nationaux/Art Resource, NY)

been to Corinth, but perhaps someone had been to Jerusalem and heard him speak, or had heard of him from another source who was impressed. Some interpreters view this as a faction of Judiazers within the congregation, but the only evidence comes from the prohibition against eating food previously offered to idols. Chapters 8–10, however, say that these people were accustomed to idols and were obviously Gentiles.[1]

Even that was not enough for some in the church! There was still another group. These were the back-to-Jesus folks. They were the people Paul quotes as saying, "I belong to Jesus." They weren't interested in the new religion. If the old one was good enough for Jesus, they figured, it was good enough for them. You have to wonder if this was a real faction within the Corinthian church or merely an example of Paul's sarcasm.

WHAT IS *REALLY* GOING ON?

It would be easy to view the situation in Corinth as a fight about "my favorite preacher," but that perspective avoids the deeper theological issues. Paul was writing to a congregation whose members lived in a particular context and had a history of philosophy and culture that weren't "Christian." Wisdom was a

---

Factions in Corinth

Many interpreters have assumed that the slogans Paul seems to recite in 1 Cor 12 signify that distinct groups with professed loyalty to different leaders actually existed in the Corinthian church and that those groups held differing theological positions. While harmony about what the disharmonious theologies were eludes such scholars, certain general characterizations have gained fairly wide acceptance. Many see the Paul group consisting of those persons who remained loyal to his leadership and who agreed with his supposedly anti-Jewish perspective about the Torah. The Peter group, then, is often characterized, largely on the basis of Gal 2 and Acts 15, as the more "Jewish" group, with a higher regard for Torah observance. The Apollos group is often seen as more inclined toward philosophical speculation, especially the type evi- denced in Hellenistic Jewish wisdom traditions. The Christ group remains more difficult to categorize, with characterizations ranging from "Judaizing" to "ultraspiritual pneumatics." The Corinthian church was undoubtedly divided, and those divisions seem to have rooted in preferences for certain leaders. We do not have clear evidence, however, of formal "parties," nor do we have sufficient information to know what theological ideas may have defined such factions. Paul's major concern seems to be not that they have adopted erroneous theologies but that they have allowed nontheological, worldly perspectives to shape their thinking and behavior.

For a thorough discussion of the different characterizations of the groups and their theologies, see Anthony C. Thiselton, *The First Epistle to the Corinthians: A Commentary on the Greek Text* (NIGTC; Grand Rapids: Eerdmans, 2000) 123–33.

leading philosophical influence. In the first century, wisdom did not mean getting straight A's; rather, it was a preference for *sophia,* the Greek worship of wisdom. This indicates the people's continuing fascination with the Greek values in their system of belief.

The Greek wisdom philosophy emphasized rhetoric—being able to argue a position in a convincing way. Apparently, Apollos's preaching style fit this mold, so some people were naturally drawn to him.

Others argued about baptism. In an old joke, some ministers get together, and the first question they ask each other is how many baptisms they've done the previous year. It's a badge of honor. The number of baptisms they've performed is a reflection of their worth as a minister.

The same thing was true in the early church. Apollos had baptized many believers, and so they discounted the work of Paul. It is easy to read Paul's response as defensive, and in some ways it is. But it also points out an important theological issue. What is the meaning of baptism? Is it a gateway into membership? Is it a hoop one jumps through in order to be a Christian? Is it an initiation rite? Is one method better or more Christian than another? I know individuals who have refused to join a church because they were told that they had to be baptized again, as if their first baptism was illegitimate. One of the deeper issues the early church faced related to the meaning of baptism. We struggle with the same issue today.

It is always easier to focus on the present problem rather than on the deeper issue. It is easier to fight about the way we baptize rather than struggle with the meaning behind the ritual. It is easier to fight about how we do Communion instead of pondering what the table means.

Surface-level questions force us to ask tougher questions—questions about theology, what we truly mean, what is really going on around us and in us. Those questions are more difficult because we can't resolve them in a twenty-minute sermon or a thirty-minute Bible study. The disconcerting truth is that in our world, with our philosophical system, we prefer "sound bite/bumper sticker theology." It works better in our elevator speech or in our talks around the water cooler. It is easier for a "Twitter" world, where people are accustomed to typing statements in 140 characters or less.

Dealing with deep questions often reveals our differences. Because of this, it is often easier to ignore the issues, especially in light of what Paul says in 1 Corinthians 1:10: "Now I encourage you, brothers and sisters, in the name of our Lord Jesus Christ: Agree with each other and don't be divided into rival groups. Instead, be restored with the same mind and the same purpose." Paul tells them to agree and to be united.

We normally read his words as saying we should all be cut from the same pattern with no difference at all. But the Greek word used here, *katartizō*, speaks of being knitted together. It is the same one Mark uses when he talks about the disciples mending their nets when Jesus called them to follow (Mark 1:19-20).[2] Mending the nets did not mean the nets were all the same. Mending did not make the holes disappear. The mending, the *katartizō*, simply ensured that the nets held together.

Paul raises a similar question for the people of Corinth and the people of our congregation today. What holds us together? Is it the pastor? The way we do worship? Our Wednesday night potluck suppers? Our mission efforts?

This is an essential question for a congregation to ask. What holds us together? It is just as important, however, to ask what "holes" are acceptable. Does everyone have to be the same, do the same, believe the same? Where do we allow holes?

WHEN BEHAVIOR TOUCHES THEOLOGY— OR VICE VERSA

The conflicts in the church at Corinth (just like conflicts anywhere else) proved that the differences were not merely theological but also socioeconomic. They were practical concerns made especially evident around the table.

It is important to remember that the early church did not have a building on the corner of Main and Oak where they gathered on Sundays at 11:00 a.m. Instead, people got together in family homes after work for a meal and worship. Most likely, these meetings occurred in the homes of wealthier members who may not have needed to work and who usually had servants available to assist with meal preparation.

The group also needed space that the wealthy could offer. Archaeological finds indicate that many homes had small dining rooms. Most meals were eaten in an outside atrium. Special friends were invited inside to dine a private space.[3]

The problem in Corinth was that people who had to work—mainly the poor—got to church late and discovered that the meal had already been consumed. Most guests had already eaten, and there was no food left. The friends of the host, those who arrived early, had enjoyed their fill of food and drink. In fact, they were getting drunk (1 Cor 11:21)!

It helps to understand that this behavior was expected in the ancient world. The host would have encouraged his guests' lavish behavior and even taken pride in it. After all, he was providing a service for those who had nothing! He was simply living out the pattern of dominance and subordination that was prevalent in his world.

Of course, that was exactly the problem. It is still a problem in our time. From the beginning, the church has been tempted to live out the culture and philosophy of the world rather than choosing a different path. Paul is talking about a new world, reminding them that the church operates with a different philosophy, lives out a different culture, and does not reflect the values of the world but rather the love of Christ, which sees no difference between rich and poor.

This is a touchy subject for us all! We must strive to be aware of the ways in which we are living out our culture rather than the gospel. As Paul writes to the Corinthians, he also demands of us, "What culture are you living out—the culture of the world or the culture of Christ?"

QUESTIONS FOR REFLECTION

1. How can conflict be good? When is conflict a problem?
2. Who have been the formative people in your church's history? How does their teaching still influence your church's decisions and beliefs?
3. Who are the people today who serve as role models or a way to measure your own faith?
4. How much diversity is in your congregation? If you had to divide your congregation, what groupings would you use (socioeconomic, length of membership, political stance, etc.)? How do the different groups interact? How do they communicate?
5. What holds your congregation together? How do you deal with your differences? How does your congregation handle conflict?
6. What disagreements, conflicts, or arguments have you experienced or known about involving the church?

NOTES

1. Gordon D. Fee, *The First Epistle to the Corinthians* (Grand Rapids MI: Eerdmans, 1987) 57–58.
2. Richard Hays, *First Corinthians* (Louisville: Westminster John Knox Press, 1997) 21.
3. Ibid., 195.

Session 2

SINCE YOU ASKED

Focal Text: 1 Corinthians 7:1-16; 8:1-13; 9:16-23; 10:23-33

I have discovered a major conspiracy in our house. The evidence? I recently tried to put on a pair of pants only to discover that someone had taken them in. *A lot!* Try as I might, I couldn't get them to fasten, even after drawing in my stomach as much as possible. What could have happened?

Then I discovered that someone was tampering also with the scales. I got on and saw a number that I wouldn't expect to see unless I was weighing small elephants. Someone was obviously playing with my mind.

My wife assured me that the evidence was not faulty.

The next painful step was to talk to Amy, a church member who is a dietician at the local hospital. "Amy, I need a menu to lose weight," I said. "Tell me what I can eat and what I can't eat." It seemed like an easy, rational, simple request!

But Amy wouldn't give me a menu. Instead, she wanted to talk about good food or, rather, foods that are good for me. She asked how many vegetables I ate each week. (French fries are vegetables, right?) She asked about my lifestyle and how much exercise I got and how much I was walking (and on and on and on).

That wasn't what I wanted. I wanted this dietician to give me a menu. I wanted her to make it simple and easy. But Amy didn't offer easy. She offered a lifestyle change.

That's what Paul is doing in 1 Corinthians. The church at Corinth wrote him a letter asking questions about spiritual practices and appropriate behaviors for Christians. "Brother Paul, we need your wisdom and advice about some problems in our church. What are we supposed to do about them?"

The church wrote with specific questions, and they wanted Paul to give the answers. But Paul refused! Even if he gave them direct answers, it wouldn't matter. It would have been like Amy giving me a diet plan. The Corinthians would have followed it for about a week and a half before they started cheating!

Paul did not want to give them answers. Instead, Paul introduced them to a new way of living that went against the prevailing philosophy. Paul did not give them answers; he gave them a different story to live.

In the first six chapters of 1 Corinthians, Paul lays the groundwork for his response. He issues a call for unity among the congregation, imploring them not to break apart into various factions. He reasserts his authority as an apostle, reminding them of his time with them and how he started a good thing in them. He does not shy away from scolding them and calling them to a higher standard. After providing this foundation, he is ready to address their questions.

NOW ABOUT WHAT YOU WROTE...

First Corinthians is a part of a series of letters that traveled between Paul and the church in Corinth. It would be wonderful to have the entire collection of letters so we might better understand Paul's response. Apparently, the most recent letter from Corinth was delivered to Paul in Ephesus by Stephanas, Fortunatus, and Achaicus (1 Cor 16:8, 15-17). It was probably a response to Paul's earlier letter, for it seems that they took exception to his position on several issues. From Paul's reply, we can infer that their questions concerned the following issues:
- Sex, marriage, and divorce
- Virgins
- Meat offered to idols
- Spiritual gifts
- The collection for the saints
- Apollos's travel plans

The people of Corinth seemed to be asking questions that began, "Why can't we . . . ?" These arose from their culture, background, and philosophy. "Everyone else can do this, Paul! Why can't we?" Their questions reveal a conflict of ideas within the church. They did not have the benefit of centuries of Christian teaching; they were making it up as they went. They were trying to mesh the various available teachings: the philosophy of the Stoics and Cynics who had a low view of the body and sexuality; a libertine strain within Christianity; their Jewish background and teachings; and the witness of Paul. These differences created conflict within the church, and so they asked for clarification from Paul. In 1 Corinthians, he addresses each issue with the same beginning—"*peri de*," or "now concerning."

Peri de Sexuality and Marriage

"The more things change, the more they stay the same." This phrase seems appropriate when it comes to sexual issues. What denomination, congregation,

---

The Phrase *peri de* in 1 Corinthians

AΩ Which of the problems addressed from 7:1 on should be included in those matters about which the Corinthians had written to Paul? The phrase *peri de* ("Now concerning . . .") appears six times (7:1, 25; 8:1; 12:1; 16:1, 12). Many interpreters have taken this phrase to mean that Paul was taking up in turn throughout the rest of the letter those issues raised in the Corinthians' letter to him. The six topics introduced in this way are sex between married partners (7:1-24), celibacy (7:23-40), eating food offered to idols (8:1–11:1), spiritual gifts (12:1–14:40), the collection for the poor (16:1-4), and a visit by Apollos (16:12).

Some have argued that other topics in chapters 7–16 not introduced by *peri de* should also be included in this group (head coverings, 11:2-16, and bodily resurrection, 15:1-58). Margaret Mitchell has pointed out, however, on the basis of the use of the phrase in other ancient writings, that *peri de* may simply indicate that Paul was moving from one topic to another, not that he was responding to a particular list of issues raised by the Corinthians. David Hall has observed, on the other hand, that in no other letter did Paul use the phrase so many times and that the impression it gives of Paul's responding to a list posed by the Corinthians remains probable. Paul's reference to plural matters (*hōn*) in 7:1 suggests that he meant more than only what he addressed in chapter 7. There the primary focus is on marriage relationships, with allusions to other issues such as circumcision and slavery being tangential to the main issue. Most likely, at least some of the other matters addressed in chapters 8–16 had been raised by the Corinthians' letter. Furthermore, as J. C. Hurd noted some time ago, Paul's manner of dealing with the matters that he had heard about differed sharply from his manner of treating those items that may have been included in the Corinthians' letter. This latter group (those matters that Paul treated in a calmer tone and with more sensitivity to the Corinthians' struggles) includes the very topics Paul introduced with *peri de*, which supports viewing those matters as ones included in the Corinthians' letter to Paul. Anthony Thiselton, in the most comprehensive commentary on 1 Corinthians in English, has argued that Hurd's criteria for distinguishing between Paul's different responses to his different sources remain useful.

David Hall, *The Unity of the Corinthian Correspondence* (JSNTSup 251; London: T & T Clark Int., 2003) 60.

John Coolidge Hurd Jr., *The Origin of 1 Corinthians* (Macon GA: Mercer University Press, 1983) 61–94.

Margaret M. Mitchell, "Concerning περὶ δε in 1 Corinthians," *NovT* 31 (1989): 229–56.

Anthony C. Thiselton, *The First Epistle to the Corinthians: A Commentary on the Greek Text* (NIGTC; Grand Rapids: Eerdmans, 2000) 34–36.

family, or individual is *not* wrestling with sexuality in our day? Whether homosexuality, sexual abuse, teen pregnancy, divorce, single parenthood, or hyper-sexualized media, we are awash with prickly issues that seem to have no single answer and involve many ramifications. Some claim that this is a sign of the end times.

Those folks probably need to read Corinthians. Many of the same issues were swirling around in the first century. The city of Corinth had a reputation of being hyper-sexualized, where anything and everything was possible and permissible. As we have seen, much of this was based on reputation instead of reality, but the questions still arose. How do we make decisions about our sexuality? The Corinthians raised this concern in their letter to Paul.

Some of us consider Paul anti-women and anti-sex, and this attitude can color our reading of his response. It is important for us to consider his words carefully and remember that he is responding to particular questions from a particular church. He is not writing a treatise about sexuality and marriage. In fact, when read carefully, we might discover that Paul had a rather progressive view for the first century![1]

In 1 Corinthians 7:1, Paul writes, "Now, about what you wrote [*peri de*]. 'It's good for a man not to have sex with a woman.'" Note the quotation marks around the statement about sex. Paul is quoting something that the Corinthians wrote to him. Apparently, some people in the Corinthian church took the stance that sex was completely taboo, even for married couples. They quoted the well-known line (both in the early church and for many today), "It is good for a man not to touch a woman." As indicated in our biblical translation for this study, the Common English Bible, "to touch a woman" was another way to speak about sexual relations.

Some people in the church believed that ordinary married life was incompatible with their new spiritual identity. They believed that abstaining from sex was necessary—even after they were married!

It may sound strange to us that Paul told married couples that they should have sex. To many of us, that seems like a natural occurrence for people who are married. But ascetic ideas were common in the ancient world; Stoics and Cynics argued about whether it was acceptable for philosophers to marry or whether the single life was better for the goals of the spirit. In Greek religions, virginity and sexual purity were associated with people who had given their life in service of the gods. Sexual abstinence was viewed as a means to personal wholeness and spiritual piety. When the early Christians encountered such ideas in their culture, many of them adopted the ideas as a part of their faith.

This applied to both males and females. The idea of no more sex was appealing to women who suddenly had a new level of authority and freedom within the church. Many functioned as leaders, freed from the restraints of domestic life and the limitations of pregnancy.[2] As for the men, some of them viewed their wives' insistence on abstinence as an excuse to visit prostitutes.

Paul used this information as a starting point to argue against the Corinthians' reasoning. He said that married couples must not declare a moratorium on sex. Such a stance can lead to sexual immorality. If they want to abstain for a time for the purpose of prayer, that is acceptable, but it's an unhealthy practice in the long term.

Readers often miss Paul's second point. He reminds the Corinthians that a wife doesn't have control over her body. In the ancient world, this statement indicated the norm; wives, after all, were considered their husbands' property. But Paul goes further and states that husbands don't have control of their bodies, either. This authority falls to their wives (1 Cor 7:3-4). *This* statement was extraordinary!

Temptation

Lovis Corinth (1858–1925). *Paradise*, 1911–1912. Oil on canvas. Private Collection. (Credit: Visual Arts Library/Art Resource, NY)

In Lovis Corinth's depiction of Adam and Eve in Paradise, the serpent waits in the background for the chance to tempt the couple and destroy their blissful existence. The primordial image of Satan's taking advantage of moments of weakness, especially in matters of sex, lies in the conceptual background of Paul's concern about prolonged abstinence in marriage.

It challenged the ancient view, and it can challenge our view today as well. Marriage is not a hierarchy where one person is dominant and calls all the shots. It is not an independent relationship where either person can do as he or she wishes without regard for the other. Instead, Paul affirms that marriage involves mutual submission. Neither party has the privilege of demanding. Rather, both are called to share the gift of their lives and their bodies with each other.

Next, Paul addresses several specific situations that concern the church. First, he mentions the issue of widowers and widows (1 Cor 7:8-9). In a comment that seems personal, he says, "I'm telling those who are single and widows that it's good for them to stay single like me." Does this statement hint that Paul was once married? In later rabbinic teaching, we read, "He who is 20 years old and not yet married spends all his days in sin."[3] It is likely that the Corinthians knew Paul's marital history, and so he did not need to tell them anything more about this—even though we might wish he had!

Many times, Paul seems like he's against marriage. After advising readers to stay single, he adds, "But if they can't control themselves, they should get married, because it's better to marry than to burn with passion" (1 Cor 7:9). Does Paul think that marriage is an inferior way

> **Mutuality of Bodies**
>
> Paul's argument that husbands and wives have mutual rights and responsibilities in regard to their bodies resembles the perspective expressed in some philosophical writings of the period.
>
> Musonius Rufus (AD 30–100) wrote in his *What Is the Chief End of Marriage?*, "The husband and the wife, he used to say, should come together for the purpose of making a life in common and of procreating children, and furthermore of regarding all things in common between them, and nothing peculiar or private to one or the other, not even their own bodies."
>
> Hierocles, a Stoic philosopher from the time of Hadrian (AD 117–138), according to an excerpt from the 5th-century anthologist Johannes Stobaeus, wrote, "Whereby they agree with one another to such an extent and have everything in common even to the point of their own bodies— even more, their own souls themselves."
>
> M. Eugene Boring, Klaus Berger, and Carsten Colpe, eds., *Hellenistic Commentary to the New Testament* (Nashville: Abingdon Press, 1995) 409.

> **Burning Passion**
>
> According to Dale Martin, "The reference to burning [in 1 Cor 7:9] could be taken to refer to both the fire of desire and the fire of judgment; one could read both senses in Sirach 23:16: 'Hot passion that blazes like a fire will not be quenched until it burns itself out; one who commits fornication with his near of kin will never cease until the fire burns him up' (NRSV). Although it is not entirely clear what the second 'burns' refers to (and it could simply be a parallel to the first), it could have been read, especially by an apocalyptic Jew, as promising the fires of eschatological judgment."
>
> Dale B. Martin, *The Corinthian Body* (New Haven: Yale University Press, 1995) 292 n39.

of life? Probably not, but it does seem that he prefers that those who are not married—either single or widowed—remain that way. He applies this same logic to slaves—that they should remain as they are. More important than understanding *what* Paul says is understanding *why* he says it.

Paul sees everything through his eschatological lens. "Eschatology" is the theological word for what we believe about the future. Where are we headed? What will happen in the end? What pulls us forward? Paul believed that he and his contemporaries were living in the last days. He thought that Jesus would soon come back to bring in the kingdom of God on earth. This was a widespread belief. In the Gospel of John, we find the idea that John would be alive when Jesus returned (John 21:22-23). This end-of-days concept shaped Paul's words to the church. Since Jesus' return would happen soon, why be distracted by life issues? He realized that major life changes like marriage took time, energy, and attention that were better spent preparing for the coming return of Jesus.

Those of us with families know how draining they can be. How much time does your family require on a weekly basis? Getting groceries, doing the laundry, driving carpool, making sure homework is done, fixing supper—these life issues take time. How often have you said no to helping with a ministry project due to lack of time? It isn't an irresponsible answer; it's an honest response!

That is the heart of Paul's point: some things are more important than others right now because Christ will be back any day. Paul's eschatology, his view of the end of the story, heavily shaped his ethic.

As we make decisions concerning sexuality today, we need to have a similar perspective. What is the reasoning behind a particular stance? Is it shaped by our belief in Christ's return, or do we simply buy into the stance of our culture?

When is sex acceptable? This is not just an ancient biblical question. It is a major issue in our world and churches. We need to have a serious conversation that goes beneath the surface to ask the meaningful questions, the ethical questions, the "why" questions. Why is an act acceptable or unacceptable? How does our faith shape our views, or do we allow our views to shape our faith?[4] Paul reminds us that our actions matter, but, if our faith is to remain alive, we cannot neglect the reasons behind what we do.

Peri de Meat Offered to Idols

When I leave the office, I often call home to see if I need to pick up anything on my way. I pass the grocery store, and sometimes my family needs some last-minute items before dinner. "Can you pick up some chicken for supper?"

In the ancient world, the grocery store was not around the corner, but a temple might be. When an animal was sacrificed, not everything was burned on the altar. Some meat was available to eat. The priests were not only the religious leaders; they also served as butchers. Many people went to the temple to get their meat.

This practice raised a serious concern for the people in Corinth. "Can we eat this meat?" they wondered. "Is it okay to eat food that has been offered to the gods?" In 1 Corinthians 8 and 10, Paul addresses this question.

In other early Christian writings, the answer is "No!"[5] Eating meat offered as a sacrifice to idols was a hot-button issue, not because the idols had power but because the practice led to larger concerns. It raised the issue of the relationship between the

Types of Food Offered to Idols

The sanctuary of Demeter on the Acrocorinth. (Credit: Scott Nash)

In 1994 Nancy Bookidis led an archaeological excavation in the sanctuary of Demeter and Kore on the lower, north slope of the Acrocorinth that involved the analysis of flora and fauna finds. Having already determined in earlier excavations that the site contained numerous large dining facilities during the Classical and Hellenistic (but not Roman) periods, the aim of the analysis was to identify what was consumed. Most of the food eaten on site was similar to regular, domestic fare, but given the setting and what is known about the rituals of Demeter worship, it is likely that much of the food had religious significance even if it was not part of an actual sacrifice. Plant finds identified included wheat, barley, grape, fig, and olive. Animal finds included domestic pig, domestic sheep and goat, fish, and sea urchin. The numerous rodent and reptilian bones also found were from natural residents of the site presumably not used in meals. Except for the absence of bovine remains, the finds at the site are similar to what would be found in most religious settings where food was consumed. The focus of the analysis of flora and fauna remains at the sanctuary of Demeter and Kore was on the Classical and Hellenistic periods, the periods when ritual dining was known to have occurred on a large scale. The results, however, reinforce what is known about food offerings in all periods, including the early Roman. Food offered to idols included much more than meat.

Nancy Bookidis et al., "Dining in the Sanctuary of Demeter and Kore at Corinth," *Hesperia* 68 (1999): 1–54.

church and the pagan culture. It strained the relationship between social classes. It sparked questions about knowledge and love.

We rarely deal with such questions. Yet a friend who is serving overseas faced it. He was attending a dinner at the home of a friend who was not Christian. As they prepared to sit down, the host, being sensitive to my friend's Christian faith, noted that the meat had been offered as a sacrifice and asked if he could eat it. Our friend, surprised by both the question and the sensitivity, responded in a very Paul-like way. "Actually, we can!" he said. "Our Scripture says so." (It does pay to listen during Sunday school.)

Most of us will never be asked about meat offered to idols, but we still have to struggle with what it means to be Christian in a non-Christian culture. The fastest-growing subset in our country is the "nones," those with no religious affiliation. More and more people describe themselves as "spiritual but not religious," having cast aside the traditional moorings of faith. Sundays and Wednesdays no longer have cultural privilege as other groups impose on that traditionally "sacred" time.

As our world becomes more diverse, the question will not be "Can you eat meat sacrificed to idols?" as much as "What groups can you join and still be Christian?" (Can you be a Mason and be Christian? What about a member of the ACLU? The NRA? How about supporting Planned Parenthood? Can you be a member of a sorority or fraternity? Can you play on a sports team that has games on Sunday morning?)

What dividing lines will we draw?

The issue about meat and idols revealed another divide in the Corinth church—that of social class. The wealthier members would have been "forced" to network with others in Corinth who did not share their religious views. To be invited to a meal and not eat would be rude to their host.

On the other hand, for many poorer members who did not often get to eat meat, consuming meat from the temples would have been viewed as evil. This discrepancy revealed the difference in educational level as well. Paul seems to teach them by saying that "a false god isn't anything in this world," and that "there is no God except for the one God" (1 Cor 8:4). Such idols have no power.

In the end, it comes down to a balance between your knowledge and your love for others. What are you willing to give up for others, for the body of Christ? Time and again, Paul shifts to the plural, reminding the Corinthians that this is not an individual enterprise. They are called to build up the whole body of Christ! They are called to do everything for the glory of God.

Paul doesn't give a specific response on this issue of eating meat offered to idols. Instead, he throws it back on the individual believers, giving them the responsibility of making the best choice.

I once took a youth group on a mission trip to New Orleans. On our first morning, the supervisor of the center we were serving met with our group to give us an orientation. As she finished, she reminded us, "This week, you are going to be a missionary. The question is, what kind?"

Paul challenges the church in Corinth and the church on Main Street to answer that question as well. Why do we do what we do? What does it say about us? About our church? About the body of Christ?

QUESTIONS FOR REFLECTION

1. How do make decisions on moral issues? What resources do you use? Why do you believe as you do? How do your beliefs affect your choices?
2. In 1 Corinthians 7, Paul gives advice about sex. What is Paul saying about sexuality? When is sex acceptable? What makes it that way? What makes it unacceptable? What are the differences in talking about sex then, in the early church, and talking about sex in our churches today?
3. When you take a certain stance on a particular issue, what leads you to do so? Is your stance shaped by your belief that Jesus will return, or are you more likely to base it on your culture? How does your faith shape your views? Do you ever allow your views to shape your faith?
4. In 1 Corinthians 8:1-13 and 10:23-33, Paul talks about whether to eat meat offered to pagan gods. What does Paul tell the church at Corinth? How does this conversation apply to us today? What are the ideas and practices in our culture that conflict with our Christian beliefs?
5. Read 1 Corinthians 11:1. Who is Paul's example? How can you strive to be like Christ? In your life, who shows you what Christ is like?
6. The questions Paul addresses in First Corinthians—on marriage, sexuality, and food offered to idols—were hot-button issues in the early church. How important are these issues for today's church? What are some other hot-

button issues for us? How can we use Paul's teachings to guide us in exploring those issues?

NOTES

1. Richard Hays, *First Corinthians* (Louisville: Westminster John Knox Press, 1997) 111–12.

2. Ibid., 115.

3. Ibid., 119.

4. A 2011 issue of *Christian Ethics Today* reported on the proceedings of "A [Baptist] Conference on Sexuality and Covenant" (*A Journal of Christian Ethics* 20/4 [Fall 2012]). You can read the addresses at http://christianethicstoday.com/wp/wp-content/uploads/2011/02/40680_Journal-88-Special1.pdf . This is a great starting point for individual and congregations to begin a conversation about sexuality.

5. See Acts 15:28-29; Revelation 2:14, 20; and the Didache 6:3.

Session 3

WE HAVE THESE DIFFERENT GIFTS

Focal Text: 1 Corinthians 12–14

What a mess! You can hardly use the church at Corinth as an example of what a church should aspire to be. Torn apart by disagreements about leadership and fellowship, sexual immorality, and even how to behave in worship, First Church Corinth was definitely dysfunctional.

The people argued about everything, but they rarely got to the real issues. Even today, few churches have that much courage. The fights that threatened the church at Corinth still infest our churches. How can we deal with socio-economic differences between churches and even within churches? What do we do about an educational chasm? Can we address differences in thought and belief?

Too often, we take the easy solution. We customize our world to fit our preferences and our comfort. We customize our news, reinforcing our bias, dividing our world into Fox people, MSNBC people, and CNN people. We make decisions based on what suits our schedule and our taste. We turn ourselves into the center of our world, and then we wonder why people can't get along!

As Paul sought to address the Corinthians' issues, he did not give them answers as much as he called them to a different way of life. Unlike the rest of society, Paul reminds them that they are to live under another set of rules. They are to see themselves as a part of something much larger—the Body of Christ.

This idea did not begin with Paul. Like many preachers, he uses an image familiar to his readers—this time from the world of politics. He reminds them that while they may disagree and have diverse opinions and ideas, they are still one body.

Epictetus, a first- and early second-century Greek philosopher and teacher, was noted for the consistency and power of his ethical thought. He focused on integrity, self-management, and personal freedom. He reminded his disciples, "What then is the promise of a citizen? Not to take what is advantageous for him as a private individual, not planning so to be released from anything, but rather like a hand or foot if it had rational abilities and could understand the natural constitution, would never be eager or stirred up to do anything other than referring to the whole."[1] Epictetus thought of Roman citizenship as a body in which everyone worked for the good of the whole.

While this was a common idea in Paul's time, Paul takes it to another level by reminding the Corinthians that their state of being a whole body does not come with their citizenship as Romans; its source is something far more important—their baptism into the kingdom of God. "For just as the body is one and has many members," he writes, "and all the members of the body, though many, are one body, so it is with Christ. For in the one Spirit we were all baptized into one body—Jews or Greeks, slaves or free—and we were all made to drink of one Spirit" (1 Cor 12:12, NRSV).

This is important—their citizenship through baptism is above anything that might separate them. Their political views, their ethnic differences, and their social status are all cancelled out by their baptism in Christ. Being one in the Spirit is the great equalizer!

Beyond that, however, Paul makes the point that their diversity and differences actually make the church body healthier. The variety within the congregation comes from God. Paul assures the Corinthians that there is a diversity of gifts *but the same Spirit.* There is a diversity of service *but the same Lord.* There is a diversity of activities *but the same God.* He builds on a Trinitarian formula—Spirit, Lord, and God—to drive home his point that the diversity and differences are God's gifts to the church.

Too often we sing, "We are one in the Spirit," and believe that this means we are all alike. Sometimes we think we should be! But Paul says that diversity creates a healthy, living church. Our differences are essential.

But how do we live with them?

Our Need for the "Other"

The existence of "others" is not something to remove or simply overcome but to live through because we may learn from them Christ-like manifestations. In an individualistic faith and life context today, what is at stake is how to reconstruct a community for "all"—in which the rich and the poor, the happy and the unhappy, gather together in acknowledging others, comforting and being comforted, challenging and being challenged.

Yung Suk Kim, *Christ's Body in Corinth: The Politics of a Metaphor* (Minneapolis: Fortress Press, 2008) 90.

PERI DE SPIRITUAL GIFTS

Recall from session 2 that in 1 Corinthians, Paul addresses each of the congregation's issues with the same beginning—"*peri de*," or "now concerning." In 1 Corinthians 12:1, he returns to that familiar transition and says that he wants to talk to his readers about spiritual things. Perhaps Paul had heard about fights in the church over spiritual gifts. The very gifts that God had given them were dividing their fellowship. They argued about who had what gift and which gift was the most important. Each person wanted to have the "best" gift and be considered the most spiritual. In fact, some believers accused others of not being spiritual at all.

> **Grumbling**
> Theodoret of Cyr offered an interesting explanation of their grumbling. In his *Commentary on the First Epistle to the Corinthians*, he wrote, "Some of the Corinthians were grumbling that they had only received the lesser spiritual gifts, when they wanted them all" (227).
>
> Published in Gerald Bray, ed., *1–2 Corinthians* (vol. 7 of ACCS NT; ed. Thomas C. Oden; Downers Grove IL: InterVarsity Press, 1999) 64.

Paul quickly discounts these arguments. He reminds the Corinthians that if they are followers of Christ, they are all spiritual people. No one can make the confession that Jesus is Lord and not be a spiritual person, for the ability to confess Christ comes from the Holy Spirit (1 Cor 12:3).

Today, we often reverse this argument. Instead of a way to boast, it becomes an excuse not to serve. Think about committee meetings you might have attended. There are plenty of good ideas, but no one will step up to lead. We hear (or give!) the excuse, "You should ask someone else. I am not a spiritual person. I just can't do that!" Before long, we believe that certain people (even ourselves) have nothing to offer the church or God.

Paul dismisses that excuse. He insists that everyone receives gifts for the good of the body of Christ. And to make sure we understand, he gives us a list in 1 Corinthians 12:4-10:

- A word of wisdom is given by the Spirit to one person
- A word of knowledge to another according to the same Spirit
- Faith to still another by the same Spirit
- Gifts of healing to another in the one Spirit
- Performance of miracles to another
- Prophecy to another
- The ability to tell spirits apart to another

- Different kinds of tongues to another
- The interpretation of the tongues to another

Then Paul writes, "All these things are produced by the one and same Spirit who gives what he wants to each person" (v. 11). This is not meant to be a complete list of the gifts God gives. Paul gives two more lists of spiritual gifts in other letters, Romans 12 and Ephesians 4:11-13. Paul also details another set of gifts in this first letter to the Corinthians (see 12:28-30). Sometimes we limit our gift to one passage of Scripture. But that misses the point! Paul is saying that God gives gifts to the body of Christ—various gifts for different people, different situations, and different locations. Focusing on the gift is falling into the same situation that affected the Corinthians—we fail to see the whole picture. Paul wants us to see how the gifts God has given each of us can assist the whole church.

Looking beyond the "list" is urgent for the church today. For example, how do we use the wisdom of those who can fathom a business plan or work the miracle of a computer? How do we recognize those who can speak the language of a different generation? Do they have a place in our church? Can we welcome their gifts?

Each of us is given gifts so that we can serve the body of Christ. Whenever we deny our gifts, try to make them more important, or see them as not important or needed, we harm the body of Christ. Whenever we ignore the gifts of others or place them on a pedestal above us, we harm the body of Christ. Whenever we get into arguments about what gift is more important, seeking to make ourselves more significant or to get out of a ministry opportunity, we harm the body of Christ.

Too often, this is the way we operate. So Paul gives us a more excellent way.

A MOST FAMILIAR PASSAGE

First Corinthians 13 is perhaps the most well-known passage in the Bible. Even people who wonder what a John 3:16 sign at a football game means may recognize 1 Corinthians 13 as the love passage that is often read at weddings.

Our youngest daughter, who, as a preacher's kid, has been to more than her fair share of weddings, can no longer listen to the passage without making a joke. She wants to turn it into a rap:

> Love is patient,
> Love is kind,
> But this poem
> It does not rhyme!

Even without rhyme, though, Paul's words are poetic. Some scholars connect 1 Corinthians 13 to Plato's longer writing on *eros* love.[2] Plato writes in the *Symposium* (dated 385–380 BC),

> Love fills us with togetherness and drains all our divisiveness away . . . love moves us to mildness, removes from us wildness. He is giver of kindness, never of meanness . . . father of elegance, luxury, delicacy, grace, yearning, desire. Love cares well for good men, cares not for bad ones. In pain, in fear, in desire, or speech, Love is our best guide and guard; he is our comrade and our savior. Ornament of all gods and men. Every man should follow Love, sing beautifully his hymns.[3]

This passage was probably familiar to the city's elite, and Paul may have used it as an way to refocus them on the new way of living that he was teaching.

Paul begins by reminding his readers of the various gifts he has addressed, which the members of the Corinthian church may have viewed as the most important: speaking in tongues, prophecy, knowledge of mysteries, mountain-moving faith, generosity that gives away everything, and giving up one's own body. This is an impressive list! Paul is not seeking to discredit these gifts. He simply wants to remind the Corinthians that these gifts are worthless on their own. While they are wonderful gifts, the way of love is the opposite of how the people are acting. Love calls them to live differently. John Calvin observed, "I have no doubt that Paul intended I Corinthians 13 to reprimand the Corinthians in an indirect way, by confronting them with a situation quite the reverse of their own, so that they might recognize their own faults by contrast with what they saw."[4] For a church so divided, Paul saw love as the cure.

In a world with multiple words for love—*eros, philia, agape*—Paul focuses on describing the love that people should live out in the church. He does not write about *eros*, which means romantic love. Nor does he use *philia*, which indicates the love between friends. Instead, he uses *agape*, a self-giving love.

First, Paul gives two positive qualities of *agape* love. Love is "patient" and "kind." Love is both passive and active in how it responds to others (13:4). Once again, he reminds the Corinthians that church is not a solitary enterprise. Patience and kindness are necessary for living in community, but, even more, they represent the qualities of God, which he has described in other letters (see Rom 2:4).

A list of negatives comes next. Paul tells his readers what love is *not*. Most of these negative qualities are seen in the life of the Corinthian church. It is as if Paul were saying, "If you are a Christian, you have to behave the opposite of your current behavior!"[5]

Love "isn't jealous" (1 Cor 13:4). Love does not allow fellow believers to have rivalries with each other. This probably reflects those who stand against Paul and cause discord because they prefer someone else's teachings. Love, he insists, is not concerned with what *I* want but rather with what will best serve *others*.

Love "doesn't brag" (v. 4). Paul rarely uses this word. Bragging or boasting means to behave as a braggart or to be a windbag. It suggests self-centered actions that call attention to an individual. This kind of behavior is impossible if one is most concerned with the well-being of the whole community.

Love "isn't arrogant" or proud (v. 4). The word means "to be puffed up." For Paul,

Venus before a Mirror

Peter Paul Reubens. *Venus before a Mirror*. 1614–1615. Oil on wood. Sammlung Fùrst von Liechtenstein, Vaduz Liechtenstein. (Credit: Erich Lessing/Art Resource, NY)

Reubens's portrayal of Venus, goddess of love, captures her vainly observing her reflection in the mirror. Paul's portrayal of love stresses, by contrast, that love is not conceited or arrogant. Later, in v. 12, he also points out that we see only indirectly with a mirror and cannot yet know God as we are known by God.

this is the Corinthians' great sin: they are arrogant, and they have no reason to be. Their behavior is unholy.[6]

Love "isn't rude" (v. 5). The KJV translates this verse as "love doth not behave itself unseemingly." Though outdated, this translation says that love cares for others too much to act in a disgraceful way.

Love "doesn't seek its own advantage" (v. 5). This is an echo from earlier in the letter where Paul spoke of eating whatever one wanted to eat. In that discussion, Paul reminded the Corinthians that they should seek the good of all. Love always seeks the best for everyone involved.

Love "isn't irritable," and love "doesn't keep a record of complaints" (v. 5). Here, Paul begins to move beyond the situation in Corinth. He suggests that love gives us patience and the ability to hold back our anger. This idea takes readers back to where the list began—with being patient and kind.

Love "isn't happy with injustice, but it is happy with the truth" (v. 6). These are two balanced sides of the same reality. Paul reflects on the character of God, who never rejoices over evil—whether it is war, oppression, or the failures of another. Rather, love, like God, always seeks justice and mercy, even for those with whom one disagrees.

Paul summarizes the list with these words: "Love puts up with all things, trusts in all things, hopes for all things, endures all things" (v. 7). This idea should govern the life of a community today. It is what will govern the lives of everyone when God's kingdom is fulfilled. Now we catch only a glimpse of what that is like, but then it will be the norm. Paul holds out this hope to the people of Corinth—and to us.

BACK TO PRACTICAL MATTERS

The beauty of chapter 13 is sandwiched between the practical concerns of the Corinthian church. After the love poem, Paul returns to praxis: how *agape* is lived out in the daily life of the church. He urges the believers to pursue love. That is his hope.

But there are times when we feel that we need a "how-to" manual. How should we deal with various gifts and individuals in the church? Which person and what gift gets priority? Some people may decide that everyone else's gifts are best while they choose not to serve, but others may push to the front of the line, demanding that they get the place of honor. How do we decide?

In 1 Corinthians 14, Paul gives practical advice. He begins with the gift of speaking in tongues, which seems to be the pressing issue in the Corinthian church. Paul's standard for judging the usefulness of a gift is to see how it builds up the body of Christ. While it may be impressive to speak in tongues, and it may bring attention to the one who speaks, it does nothing for the larger body unless someone can interpret what is said.

The same is true today. Some people "speak in tongues" of Bible talk, theology points, and even church terms. They sound impressive, but how do they help those sitting in the pews, in the classroom, in the world? The goal is not the individual; it's the whole. Seven times in the fourteenth chapter, Paul uses the verb *oikodomein* ("to build up") or the noun *oikodomē* ("upbuilding," "edification"). The gauge of a spiritual gift is how well it builds the body of Christ.

With that in mind, Paul the great theologian becomes the traffic cop. He recognizes that everyone brings gifts to the work of the church. Each person has a hymn she wants to sing, a Scripture he wants to share, a revelation, a word from God. But everyone can share at the same time—together. The guideline is the same: do what builds up the body of Christ.

> **Zeal for Spirits**
>
> AΩ 1 Cor 14:12 literally reads, "Since you are zealots of spirits (*pneumatōn*), for [the purpose of] the edification of the church seek so that you might abound." The statement is worded in such a way that the object of "abound" is unclear. Most interpreters understand Paul to mean that they should strive to abound *for the edification of the church*. This certainly fits the thrust of Paul's argument throughout. The syntax of the sentence, however, also allows for understanding the assumed object to be "spirits." Thus, the sense would be, "Since you are zealots of [i.e., for] spirits, for the edification of the church, strive to abound [*in spirits*]. "Spirits" would be understood in this case as external spirits that inspire speech, both *glossolalia* and prophecy. Most interpreters also hold that the word that literally means "spirits" should be read as essentially equivalent to *pneumatika* ("spiritual things"). If so, one wonders why Paul did not use *pneumatika* instead of *pneumatōn*. Translating *pneumatōn* as "spirits" is more in keeping with its normal meaning and probably more accurately reflects the Corinthians' perspective. They were seeking to be inspired by "spirits" that would empower them to speech in tongues. That may be one reason stressed that Paul stressed in 12:4-10 that it is the *one* Spirit that lies behind all gifts. Taking "spirits" as the object of "abound," however grammatically possible, misses Paul's point, which is that their zeal should be directed toward the things that will edify the church.
>
> Clint Tubbs, "The Spirit (World) and the (Holy) Spirit among the Earliest Christians: 1 Corinthians 12 and 14 as a Test Case," *CBQ* 70 (2008): 324–25.

ABOUT *THOSE* VERSES

If 1 Corinthians 13 is the most well-known chapter, 1 Corinthians 14:34-35 may be the most difficult passage. If only Paul had known the division these verses would cause. How many churches have argued over the words, "women should be quiet during the meeting" (v. 34)? It seems as if this advice goes against everything Paul has already said to the Corinthians. They don't seem to fit. Many ancient manuscripts place these verses as an addendum at the end of the chapter, and one manuscript includes markings suggesting that the scribe considered them a gloss inserted into the text.[7] After all, we do not have Paul's original letters; we have copies of copies of copies. Some scholars believe that these verses in chapter 14 were notes that a scribe wrote on the edge of his copy that eventually made their way into the manuscript.

Scholar Gordon Fee brings up several other difficulties. The verses contradict 1 Corinthians 11:2-16, where it seems that women are praying and prophesying in the assembly. Other writings show that women played an active role in preaching, teaching, and prophesying in the early church (for example, Phoebe [Rom 16:1-2], Prisca [Rom 16:3-4], Euodia and Syntyche [Phil 4:2-3]). Fee also notes that the language used in these verses is unlike Paul's.[8] Because of these issues, many scholars do not think that Paul himself wrote these words.

But they are in the text, and we must decide what to do with them. Some treat them like a text as important as John 3:16. They have become the way of dividing churches—even though Paul's entire goal is to unite believers. Another temptation is to ignore them. (I will confess that was a rather appealing option as we wrote this chapter!)

Maybe we should read them in the tension of the text. Scripture doesn't always confirm itself.[9] The Bible is an ancient text with its own culture and history. The words in 1 Corinthians 14:34-35 reflect the culture of the first century, and most women would have not have thought they were being oppressed. Instead, these words were another way to avoid disorder in worship.

Our culture today is different. The same social codes do not apply, as women serve in leadership roles in business, government, and the church. Congregations must recognize that we cannot afford to deny the gifts that females have to offer. They are much needed today! And besides, giving women the opportunity to serve and to share is a loving action that builds up the body of Christ.

QUESTIONS FOR REFLECTION

1. What do you know about spiritual gifts? What gifts does Paul list in 1 Corinthians 12:4-11? In Romans 12:6-8, Paul gives us another list. What gifts can we add to the list? If you were writing a list today, what other gifts would you include?
2. How does the variety in people's backgrounds and gifts create a healthy church?
3. Consider the faithful Christians you have known. Can you name people in your church or in other circles of your life who had a certain gift? How did that person live out his or her gift? How was it used in community?
4. What gifts can you recognize in yourself? How can you use them to build up the body of Christ?
5. Read 1 Corinthians 13 aloud, but begin with 1 Corinthians 12:31. This passage is often read at weddings, and its concept of love is applied to marriage and family. But how does the meaning change when we think about it in the context of using our gifts in community and striving for the "even better way" of love?

NOTES

1. Quoted in Pheme Perkins, *First Corinthians* (Grand Rapids MI: Baker Academic, 2012) 149.

2. Ibid., 154.

3. Perkins, *First Corinthians*, 154, quoting Plato, Symposium 197d-e (trans. Nehamas and Woodruff, 1989, 37).

4. Quoted in Richard Hays, *First Corinthians* (Louisville KY: John Knox Press, 1997) 222.

5. Gordon D. Fee, *The First Epistle to the Corinthians* (Grand Rapids MI: Eerdmans, 1987) 637.

6. Ibid., 638.

7. Hays, *First Corinthians*, 246.

8. Fee, *First Epistle to the Corinthians*, 702.

9. Hays, *First Corinthians*, 248.

Session 4

THE END IS THE BEGINNING

Focal Text: 1 Corinthians 15–16

Maybe it's my age, but I'm starting to spend more time reading the middle of the local section of the newspaper: the obituaries. I find myself reading them in the morning. I read them partly out of hope that I don't know any of the names and partly out of theological inquiry.

I have said that if I ever went to school to earn another advanced degree (I am 125 percent sure that I will not!), the title of my dissertation would be "The Theology of Obituaries." Obituaries, whether intentional or not, say a lot about what we believe about death and what happens beyond the grave.

Recently I have seen these entries (names are changed):
- Louise Owens Brown, widow of Terry Robert Brown, Sr., died January 19
- Francis William Harris, 92, widower of Mary W. Harris, died peacefully
- Barbara Jackson Abernathy, 83, loving mother, passed away February 4
- Mary Etta Hill Brown, 90, widow of Allen Henry Brown, entered into eternal rest
- Blair S. Hutto, 89, left his life on earth
- William Douglas Dilligard, 46, departed this life
- Robert M. "Jake" Jacobs, Jr., 52 years young, went to be with his Heavenly Father on Friday
- Erma Delores Jones went to be with the Lord
- The relatives and friends of Mr. Walter Smalls are respectfully invited to attend his funeral service

Most obituaries are a few short lines in the newspaper written by a grieving family or by an overworked attendant who is ready to go home. But these brief lines say a lot about what we believe about death. There is a difference between "died," "left the earth," and "went to be with the Lord." These different perspectives are not only in the obituaries; they are also in our churches. We rarely ask the question, "What happens after we die?" There are so many different ideas that we don't want to take the time to debate them.

Even knowing about the resurrection, some people still believe that death is the end of the story. When you die, you are dead. Period. Others take the opposite approach, believing that the soul, the essence of an individual, is immortal and immediately goes to be with Jesus. Still others believe that individual spirits wait for judgment day, for the rapture, for something. They are in limbo.

We find sources for these varied ideas in all parts of life. Consider Charles Dickens's *A Christmas Carol.* Have you ever wondered how the ghost of Marley shapes your view of the afterlife? What about stories of the Greek gods that are continuously revised in modern tales? And think about the shows and films you have seen that address the afterlife. From *All Dogs Go to Heaven* to *Meet Joe Black* to *The Walking Dead,* questions about what happens next abound.

How often have you asked or heard someone ask, "Will we know each other in heaven?" "Will we have the same body?" What will eternity be like?" "Will we really have wings and harps and sing all the time?"

How can we answer those questions? There isn't an answer. We don't know! Yet we often give answers after people die because we don't know what else to say. We want to comfort those who grieve, but sometimes our answers make the situation worse. Early in my career, I attended a funeral service for a man named Robert, who had left behind three teenage children. These kids sat alone on the front row, as they each had a different mother and none of the mothers felt comfortable sitting with the family. The pastor, an uncle, tried to provide assurance by affirming that Robert was in heaven. After all, he had made a profession of faith. But then the uncle added, "If God came to Robert right now and said, 'Do you want to stay here or go back to earth?' I know Robert would say, 'I want to stay here.'"

I know the pastor meant well, but were his words truly comforting to the three teenagers who felt all alone?

But what, then, should we say to the grieving in such times?

Answering this question has always been difficult. It was hard for the early church as well. They too heard various ideas about what happens after death. We can see some of the differences in these ancient epitaphs from the tombs of workers:

• In memory of Viccentia, a very nice girl, a gold-worker. She lived nine years.

- Here is my home forever. Here is a rest from toil.
- I was not. I was. I am not.[1]

The people of Corinth knew about Plato's idea of the immortality of the soul. Plato assumed that the soul was separate from the mortal body, and when the body died, the soul kept on. The same idea was common in the worship of the Egyptian goddess Isis, which involved elaborate funeral rites. Isis worshipers believed that the deceased was taken to the underworld, where he saw the gods, and then he returned to this world transformed. Like those who followed Plato's thought, these believers claimed that the soul was immortal.

Jews had several ideas about death. One stream of thought was that death meant *dead*. There was no concept of a soul separate from the body. People did not have a soul; they *were* a soul. So when a person died, she was considered dead. It was the end of her story. If anything else happened with her, it was an act of God.

Others, though, clung to the idea of resurrection. Disagreements over this concept were a major source of argument between the Sadducees and the Pharisees. The Pharisees believed in resurrection. The Sadducees denied it. These conflicting views provided the background of the controversy the Sadducees mentioned when they asked Jesus about marriage in the afterlife (see Luke 20:27-33).

The ancient world, then, was similar to ours on the issue of life after death. There was no single understanding of what happened after someone died. People had multiple ideas about the soul and its relationship to the physical world. They had differing opinions about immortality and a person's passage through the postmortem period. These views led to questions. Everyone sought the truth about the matter.

Some of the believers in Corinth were like the Sadducees, denying the resurrection. They felt that death was the end of the story. Others believed that they had already been resurrected! They had been raised to a new life in Christ and therefore thought that the old rules of good conduct no longer applied to them. They felt that they were free to live as they wanted. Paul replied to their questions, since the issues were causing conflict in their church.

REMEMBERING WHERE WE STARTED AND WHERE WE ARE GOING

The many ideas about what happens after death form the basis for Paul's points throughout 1 Corinthians. The people's actions involving issues of food, drink, and relationships show that they probably misunderstand what Paul sees as the heart of the gospel—the death and resurrection of Jesus.

Paul reminds his readers of their salvation. Their salvation is fact. It is not under dispute. Paul is reassuring his believers that they are being saved. And so Paul uses this basic truth as a starting point for giving them a refresher course about what he has already proclaimed to them (1 Cor 15:3-8):

> **Barth on 1 Corinthians 15**
> It cannot be by chance that 1 Cor. xv, the chapter which deals with the most positive subject that can be imagined, forms the very peak and crown of the essentially critical and polemically negative Epistle. What is disclosed here is Paul's key position. The Resurrection of the Dead is the point from which Paul is speaking and to which he points. From this standpoint, not only the death of those now living, but, above all, their life *this side* of the threshold of death, is in the apostolic sermon, veritably seen, understood, judged, and placed in the light of the last severity, the last hope.
>
> Karl Barth, *The Resurrection of the Dead* (Eng. trans.; London: Hodder & Stoughton, 1933) 101.

1. Christ died for our sins in line with the scriptures,
2. he was buried, and he rose on the third day in line with the scriptures.
3. He appeared to Cephas, then to the Twelve,
4. and then he appeared to more than five hundred brothers and sisters at once—most of them are still alive to this day, though some have died. Then he appeared to James, then to all the apostles,
5. last of all he appeared to me . . . .

This is an early formula of confession. Paul doesn't need to give them Scripture references any more than a pastor today needs to print the more common words of "Amazing Grace" in the bulletin. The Corinthians know the Scriptures Paul mentions by heart.

It is impossible to match Paul's account with the Gospel stories of the resurrection. Paul did not have those stories in front of him; they were not yet written. Paul does not include the tale of the women witnessing Jesus' resurrection. But Paul is not writing history. He is trying to persuade his readers of the truth of the resurrection.

By adding his experience with the risen Lord (v. 8), however, Paul directly addresses those who question his authority as an apostle. He also reminds them that he has "worked harder than all the others," though he does add that it was by the "grace of God that is with me" (v. 10). Paul is human. He is hurt by the critiques and feels the need to respond. In fact, the term he uses to describe himself, one "born at the wrong time" (v. 8), may have been a direct quote from some of his critics. The word used here, *ektrōma*, ordinarily refers to an aborted fetus. Some of Paul's detractors thought he was weak (see 2 Cor 10:10).[2] At the very least, he was considered unattractive. This is another instance in which Paul uses the words of his detractors to goad them.

> **Daniel and Resurrection**
>
> The earliest clear reference to resurrection in biblical literature appears in the book of Daniel, which was probably written in the mid-2d century BC.
>
> Many of those who sleep in the dust of the earth shall awake, some to everlasting life, and some to shame and everlasting contempt. Those who are wise shall shine like the brightness of the sky, and those who lead many to righteousness, like the stars forever and ever. (Dan 12:2-3; NRSV)

Paul argues with those who claim that there is no resurrection. He begins with their statement: "there is no resurrection." If there is no resurrection, then Christ was not raised. If Christ was not raised, then we are still in our sin and everyone who has died is destroyed. There is no hope for them. If there is no hope, then we are truly crazy to believe any of this, for we are more lost than lost!

But the Corinthians know that they are saved. They have been changed. And their salvation and transformation are based on the reality of Christ's resurrection.

A trained debater could challenge each item on Paul's list, but Paul is not trying to win an intellectual debate. He does not give a concrete explanation of how resurrection happens. He uses the image of a seed, stating that it is placed in the ground and is changed into something different. Paul has no more answers about the mystery than we do.

It is easy to get bogged down in Paul's first-century arguments. He was working against a system that has little meaning to us. In *Messiah*, musician Handel quotes Paul: "Behold, I tell you a mystery: We shall not all sleep; but we shall all be changed, In a moment, in a twinkling of an eye, at the last trumpet; the trumpet shall sound, and the dead shall be raised incorruptible, and we shall be changed."[3] These lyrics are beautiful, but few of us believe that those who have died are merely "sleeping." We know that our bodies decompose and eventually become one with the earth.

Ideas about death are different here and now than they were in the Corinth of Paul's day. In fact, if we are honest, most of us hold ideas about death that are closer to the ones Paul argues against. But he seeks to respond to those in grief. He seeks to give comfort and assurance to those who have watched their loved ones die prior to Christ's return. He seeks to give us hope.

Paul reminds us that resurrection holds creation and redemption together. Without resurrection, God simply abandons our bodies and even all of creation. Resurrection makes Christian hope real and confirms God's love for creation, both now and beyond the grave. Resurrection also gives hope to those who have suffered a loss. Paul does not discount death. It is real. He does not offer happy comments like the ones we often hear or sometimes give ("God needed her more than you do"; "He is so happy now in heaven"; "This happened for a reason"). Instead, Paul affirms the depth of our loss while offering hope that death is not the end.[4]

Paul does not give an answer to how this resurrection occurs. None of us have the words to describe what we do not know. Paul is not speaking out of facts here; he is speaking out of faith. He is not speaking with certainty; he is speaking with hope. But in the end, Paul is speaking to the Corinthians with the greatest of all spiritual gifts, *agape*—the ultimate love.

> **Chrysostom on the Dead**
>
> "Sin has brought death into the world, and we are baptized in the hope that our dead bodies will be raised again in the resurrection. If there is no resurrection, our baptism is meaningless and our bodies will remain *as dead as they are now*." (Italics added)
>
> Chrysostom, *Homilies on the Epistles of Paul to the Corinthians* 40.2, in Gerald Bray, ed., *1–2 Corinthians* (vol. 7 of ACCS NT; ed. Thomas C. Oden; Downers Grove IL: InterVarsity Press, 1999) 166.

FINAL PLANS

After these words about resurrection, Paul is ready to close his letter to the Corinthians. He has addressed their questions. All that remains is to give a few final remarks. But even these give Paul an opportunity to heal divisions.

His first instructions are about a collection for the church in Jerusalem (1 Cor 16:1-4). Paul says that that this offering isn't for him, and he does not want them to take a special offering for him when he comes. Instead, he asks that they set aside a bit each week in order to help those in Jerusalem. It is worth noting that Paul does not ask this only of the wealthy members of the congregation. He asks it of them all. Also, he mentions no structure the church could use to hold these funds until he arrives. Instead, saving the gifts is the responsibility of each family.

We aren't aware of the level of need in the Jerusalem church. Some scholars note that Queen Helena of Adiabene, a Jewish sympathizer, sent famine relief funds around this time. Saul and Barnabas are mentioned in Acts 11:27-30 as taking funds from Antioch for the purpose of helping the Jerusalem church around AD 47.[5]

Paul's Terms for the Collection

1 Cor 16:1, 2	"contribution" (*logeia*)
1 Cor 16:3	"gift" (*charin*)
Rom 15:25	"serving" (*diakonōn*)
Rom 15:26	"sharing" (*koinōnia*)
Rom 15:28	"fruit" (*karpos*)
Rom 15:31	"service" (*diakonia*)
2 Cor 8:4	"service" (*diakonia*)
2 Cor 8:6, 7, 19	"this gift" (*charin tautēn*)
2 Cor 8:20	"this generosity" (*adrotēs tautē*)
2 Cor 9:1, 13	"service" (*diakonia*)
2 Cor 9:11	"this offering" (*leitourgia tautē*)
2 Cor 9:13	"sharing" (*koinōnia*)

Paul is asking for more than an offering, however. The people's gifts to the "mother church" are a reminder—both to the Corinthians and to those in Jerusalem—that despite their origins, their practices, and even their theology, Gentile and Jewish Christians belong to the one body of Christ.

Next, Paul shares his travel plans with his friends. He is going to stay in Ephesus until Pentecost to continue the work there, even against opposition. Acts 19:21-40 gives an example of the trouble he faces in Ephesus.

In the meantime, he is sending Timothy to be with the Corinthians (1 Cor 16:10). He urges the church to welcome him warmly. Paul is concerned about how they will receive Timothy, who is bringing this letter that has taken them all to task over sexuality, worship,

Ephesus

Facing northwest down Curetes Street toward the Library of Celsus. (Credit: Scott Nash)

and spiritual gifts. It is not a happy letter, and Timothy has the responsibility of taking it to the Corinthians and leading the necessary reforms. Paul hopes that the church will support rather than oppose him.

In what may seem like a strange verse, Paul also tells the Corinthian church that he has encouraged Apollos to come and visit (v. 12). This is the same Apollos who was in competition with Paul in the minds of many in the church. Paul's invitation to Apollos was a reminder that he, Paul, was the "father" of the church and also that he and Apollos were working together. This is another practical lesson, though it is hard to live. This may be why Paul says, "Stay awake, stand firm in your faith, be brave, be strong. Everything should be done in love" (1 Cor 16:13-14).

Finally, as he closes his letter, Paul sends personal greetings from people he has met along the way. Remember that letters were the main way of communicating and sharing with others. Even more, letters like this one reminded the church that they were connected to a larger body of faith.

May that be a reminder for us all: we are part of something much larger than ourselves, larger than our congregation that meets on the corner, larger than the denomination to which we belong. We are part of the body of Christ!

CONCLUSION

Reading someone else's mail is always dangerous. You might discover something that makes you question who they are and what they are planning. But you might also learn something about yourself. Through their words, you might hear a word from God. The people of Corinth were hardly a model church—or maybe they were. They were filled with people just like us, dealing with divisions and conflicts and struggles over how to be the people of God, the body of Christ, in their world. Paul wrote to them to encourage them to live differently. He reminded them that they weren't to be like other people. They were to be the people of God.

Is that the word of God for us amid our conflicts and divisions? Let's pray that it will be!

QUESTIONS FOR REFLECTION

1. How does our culture shape what we believe about death? Name some books, TV shows, or movies that address the concept of what happens after we die. What do these sources say about death?
2. What do you believe happens after someone dies? What did the people in the church at Corinth believe about life after death?
3. Read 1 Corinthians 15:50-58 aloud. What does it mean when Paul says that we will all be changed? Do we *know* this, or do we *believe* and *hope* it will come to pass? What can we know about what happens after death?
4. Even among all the unknowns about death, where can we find comfort and peace about what lies ahead?

NOTES

1. Pheme Perkins, *First Corinthians* (Grand Rapids MI: Baker Academic, 2012) 172.

2. Richard Hays, *First Corinthians* (Louisville KY: Westminster John Knox, 1997) 258.

3. "Handel's Messiah," pt. 3, nos. 47–48, http://www.worshipmap.com/lyrics/messiahtext.html (accessed 16 Octber 2013).

4. Hays, *First Corinthians*, 278–79.

5. Perkins, *First Corinthians*, 196.

NEED MORE BIBLE STUDY MATERIAL?

The Smyth & Helwys *Annual Bible Study* is a valuable tool for teaching specific books of the Bible. It contains solid scholarship, easy-to-read Study Guides, affordable books, and is linked to the Smyth & Helwys Bible Commentary series. These undated Bible book studies each have a Teaching Guide and a Study Guide. Bundle options are available.

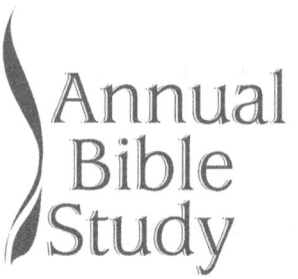

1 & 2 Samuel: Surviving the Tensions of Life by James C. Dant
Study Guide 6.00
Teaching Guide 14.00

Job: Into the Fire, Out of the Ashes by Tony W. Cartledge & Jan C. Rush
Study Guide 6.00
Teaching Guide 14.00

Proverbs: Living Wisely, Loving Well by Alicia Davis Porterfield & Eric Porterfield
Study Guide 6.00
Teaching Guide 14.00

Jeremiah: Raising Faith from the Fire by Bill Hill
Study Guide 6.00
Teaching Guide 14.00

Don't Forget the Smyth & Helwys Commentary Available for Each Study.

CHECK OUT OUR OTHER ANNUAL BIBLE STUDIES

Ezekiel: God's Presence in Performance by William D. Shiell
Study Guide 6.00
Teaching Guide 14.00

Daniel: Keeping Faith When the Heat Is On by Bill Ireland
Study Guide 6.00
Teaching Guide 14.00

Jonah: Reluctant Prophet, Merciful God by Taylor Sandlin
Study Guide 6.00
Teaching Guide 14.00

Matthew: Living as Disciples of Jesus by Guy Sayles
Study Guide 6.00
Teaching Guide 14.00

Mark: Finding Ourselves in the Story by Brett & Carol Younger
Study Guide 6.00
Teaching Guide 14.00

Luke: Parables for the Journey by Michael L. Ruffin
Study Guide 6.00
Teaching Guide 14.00

For more information call **1-800-747-3016** or visit **www.helwys.com/abs**

CHECK OUT OUR OTHER ANNUAL BIBLE STUDIES

Acts: Living with Passionate Faith
by Judson Edwards
Study Guide 6.00
Teaching Guide 14.00

Romans: The Letter that Changed Christian History by Mark J. Olson
Study Guide 6.00
Teaching Guide 14.00

1 Corinthians: Growing through Diversity by Don & Anita Flowers
Study Guide 6.00
Teaching Guide 14.00

Hebrews: Encouragement for a Life of Faith by Dalen C. Jackson
Study Guide 6.00
Teaching Guide 14.00

James: Being Right in a Wrong World by Michael D. McCullar
Study Guide 6.00
Teaching Guide 14.00

Revelation: Weaving a Tapestry of Hope by David M. May
Study Guide 6.00
Teaching Guide 14.00

For more information call **1-800-747-3016** or visit **www.helwys.com/abs**

www.ingramcontent.com/pod-product-compliance
Lightning Source LLC
Chambersburg PA
CBHW060721030426
42337CB00017B/2954